★NSYNC
★Ndepth

Maggie Marron

★NSYNC
★Ndepth

Maggie Marron

MetroBooks

Dedication

For Emily Z., my "mom"

Acknowledgments

Thanks as ever to all the great, wonderful, and talented people who keep the old Maggie machine running and spurting out books. First and foremost are the fans, who share the passion and keep the dream alive—thanks guys! And thank you, Christine Guarino Mayer for digging up stuff in places I'd never even think to look, providing me with more information than I could cram into even ten books, and for holding my hand through a difficult point in my life, all while raising two tiny kids; I would be so lost without you. Thanks also to my fabulous editor, Ann Kirby Payne, who is always there—to sign me for a book project, to be a great friend (especially when it comes to deadlines), to remind me that the most pressure comes from me, and for always believing in me. I would be remiss not to thank Shawna Mullen, the glam chick of the century, for being my eyes and helping me find the strength—not to mention, the inspiration—to go on when I needed it most. And what can I say about the next person, who played such a crucial role in transforming this project from a pile of ideas into a printable book? Jonathan Ambar, you are a pillar of pop culture passion, and without you, I could never have gotten over my writer's block and made it across the finish line. Your insights on all the guys were invaluable—and man, you write well! Last but not least, thanks to Francine Hornberger, a woman who knows me so well, I sometimes think she's my alter-ego. You know the role you play in this crazy game. If not for you, I couldn't pay my bills—let alone eat!

An Imprint of Friedman/Fairfax Publishers

Library of Congress Cataloging-in-Publication Data available upon request.

ISBN 1-58663-276-0

Editor: Ann Kirby-Payne
Art Director: Kevin Ullrich
Designer: Mark Weinberg
Photo Editor: Jami Ruszkai
Production Manager: Rosy Ngo

Color separations by Radstock Repro
Printed in England by Butler & Tanner Ltd.

1 3 5 7 9 10 8 6 4 2

For bulk purchases and special sales, please contact:
Friedman/Fairfax Publishers
Attention: Sales Department
230 Fifth Avenue
New York, NY 10001
212/685-6610 FAX 212/685-3916

Visit our website:
www.metrobooks.com

Contents

Introduction

Just when you thought it was safe to venture into the bookstore again... Well, what can I say? When you find a topic as juicy and exciting and current as 'N Sync, there's always more to be said. These boys are a constant source of interest and information for me, and I hope that you, too, just can't get enough! And I guess if you're reading this, I might just be right!!

It's hard to believe that these guys have been together now for more than half a decade, and they're showing no signs of anything except getting stronger and stronger. And the longer they stay together, the better they get! Think about it: all those songs, hours of radio-play, and countless tours, appearances, and signings. Through it all, they remain as close as brothers—despite the way their hair, their clothes, even their adorable faces have grown from cute to distinguished and oh-so-handsome. Lots of changes, and all for the better! They've lived through so much together—Justin's high school graduation, the birth of Joey's first child, all kinds of new businesses starting up—and yet, they only get closer and closer.

This book is a tribute to the guys, not just to their professional accomplishments, but to their very selves—the guys whose images plaster our bedrooms and lockers, the guys who have stolen our very hearts, the guys who sing us to sleep at night when we put their CDs on and dream away of what our lives could be if they were right there, singing us to sleep in person. Sigh...

Happy gazing!
—Maggie

> **What's your favorite 'N Sync flavor—Joey, Chris, Justin, Lance, or JC?**

CHAPTER ONE

JC 411

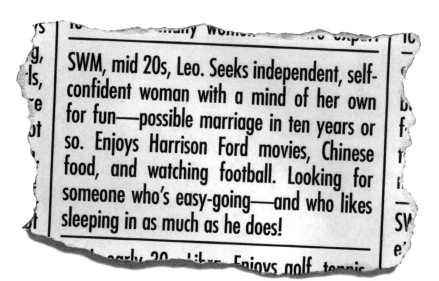

SWM, mid 20s, Leo. Seeks independent, self-confident woman with a mind of her own for fun—possible marriage in ten years or so. Enjoys Harrison Ford movies, Chinese food, and watching football. Looking for someone who's easy-going—and who likes sleeping in as much as he does!

If dreamboats were cruise ships, then this luscious Leo would be the *Titanic* (with a better track record). But there is more to JC Chasez than meets the eye. Of course, he's very pleasing to look at—why, with those deep blue peepers, killer smile, and the sexiest set of cheekbones outside of Spike on *Buffy the Vampire Slayer*, he can just stand there doing nothing and he'd still be tearin' up our hearts. Then there is that voice. Each note that emerges from his throat soars with a passion that can't be beat. And one thing he is passionate about is music. Sure, those were some H-O-T moves in the "Space Cowboy" performance during the recent *No Strings Attached* tour, but equally fiery is knowing that our boy JC co-wrote the song as well! In fact, you'll find him experimenting constantly in the studio (most likely with a

JC in an early studio shot.

Can you say prep-pie!!

keyboard and container of Chinese takeout at his side), coming up with exciting new sounds that give 'N Sync its musical edge.

Utter passion drives JC's every move. It's not about money and it's not about fame. He doesn't have a problem with these perks, but he has learned that money and fame both come with a price. Performing—it's just what you do if you're JC. "I love singing and dancing," he says, "and if I had to do it broke, I'd do it broke!"

What else about JC makes him so swoon-worthy? Maybe it's the fact that even though he admires physical beauty, ultimately that is not what impresses him in a girl. "I love exotic-looking girls. Anybody who's not afraid to be different," says JC "That's it. It's plain and simple. I don't like people who go out of their way to be different, but people who are comfortable with themselves and unafraid to do what they're feeling at that moment." No, what he's really looking for is someone with whom he can talk.

And there would be soooo much to talk to JC about! What sorts of questions would you ask? Discussing music with JC is always a good way to start things off. Did you know that he has an

JC: Head to Toe

"Do you remember Buddy Holly when he was cool like in the fifties? Well, that's what JC tries to look like."—CHRIS ON JC

Can you sum up JC-style in a word? Not really. His amazing looks are definitely one of the main ingredients, but he's got a lot more going for him than bright blue eyes and a chiseled smile. Observe:

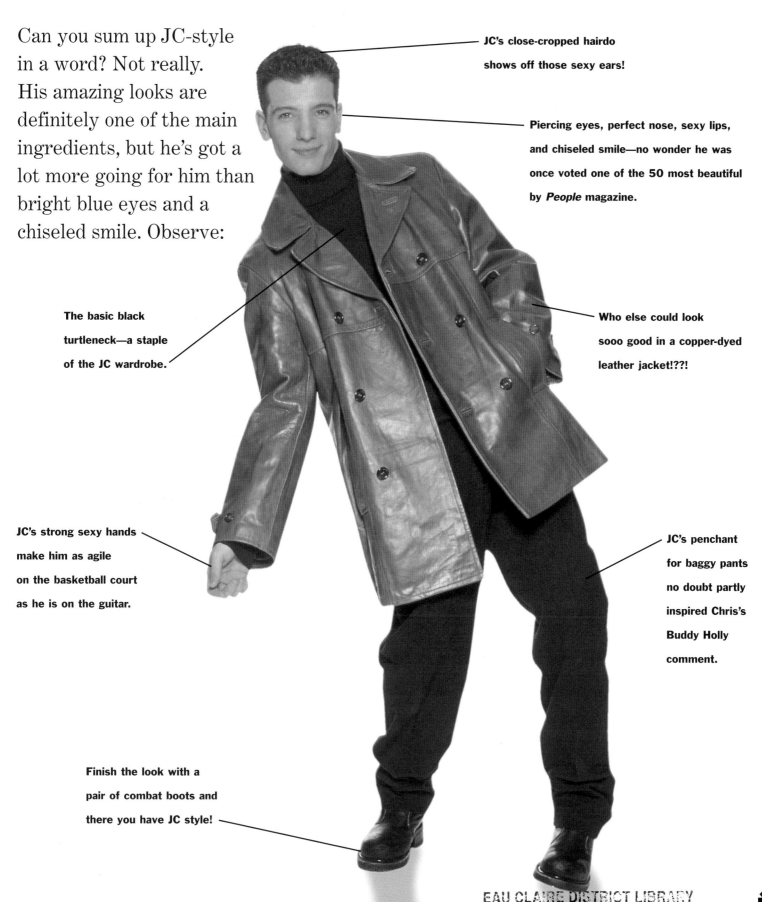

JC's close-cropped hairdo shows off those sexy ears!

Piercing eyes, perfect nose, sexy lips, and chiseled smile—no wonder he was once voted one of the 50 most beautiful by *People* magazine.

The basic black turtleneck—a staple of the JC wardrobe.

Who else could look sooo good in a copper-dyed leather jacket!??!

JC's strong sexy hands make him as agile on the basketball court as he is on the guitar.

JC's penchant for baggy pants no doubt partly inspired Chris's Buddy Holly comment.

Finish the look with a pair of combat boots and there you have JC style!

eclectic taste in tunes? Yup, when he's not composing smash pop songs, you can often find him at jazz clubs, or kicking back to mellow grooves from the likes of Harry Connick, Jr., Billie Holiday, and Sade.

JC loves music and he has a lot of respect for musicians. One of the few pet peeves this sexy crooner has, but which he doesn't let get him too down, is that some people don't take him and the guys—and especially their music—seriously. "People are going to take stabs at us because we're a boy band, regardless," he says, "so I don't even take that stuff seriously now because every time you dog a five-piece boy band, I can dog a five-piece rock band or a four-piece harmony group. I don't take that stuff literally, but what I do take literally is the stabs they take at the music."

Ask him about his cat, Grendel, and what kind of dogs he likes, because he's a total animal lover. (This is not surprising, considering what a fox he is!) His collection of Hard Rock Café menus from around the world would also spark a heated chat fest—as well as the new home in Los Angeles that he's just purchased and re-modeled. And with none other than Britney Spears as a neighbor, one wonders if he ever needs to run across the street to borrow a cup of sugar from her when he's cooking in his gourmet kitchen!

Is he looking forward to the film version of *The Lord of the Rings*? Considering that *The Hobbit* is his favorite book of all time, that very well may be the case. Could it be that behind the glamorous exterior, lies a bookworm? Hmmmmm. Well, JC is considered the most serious 'N Syncer. He's been

JC pours his heart and soul into his music.

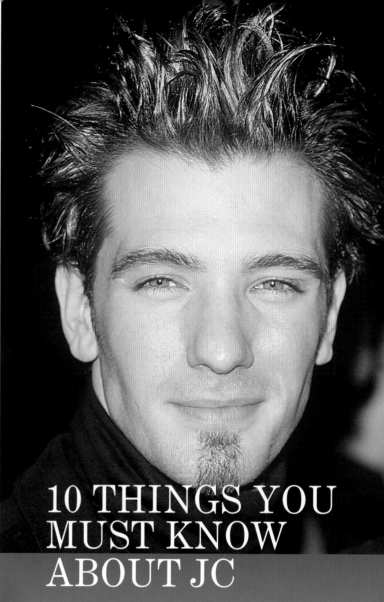

10 THINGS YOU MUST KNOW ABOUT JC

1. His first name is Joshua.

2. He grew up in Bowie, Maryland.

3. He can't watch enough TV.

4. His good luck charm is a lion necklace—he's been wearing it now for the past seven years and has never taken it off!

5. He is the least "girl crazy" of the guys. Sure, he loves looking at women, but he's more apt to notice other things as well when the guys are out, like buildings or dogs.

6. Water is his fave drink.

7. His fave sport is football.

8. The rest of the guys call him "Big Daddy," because even though he isn't the oldest, he looks out for everyone in the group. In fact, according to Chris, "He babies us."

9. He's the "serious" one.

10. He just bought a house in Los Angeles—and from his window, he can see Britney Spears's house!

*There's no question that good oral
hygiene is the secret to
that million-dollar smile, is there JC?*

Evolution of a Style:
JC, Then

JC's look may not have changed all that much, but one thing's for sure: JC gets sexier every day! Take a tour of JC's style from the early days through today and you'll see what I mean!

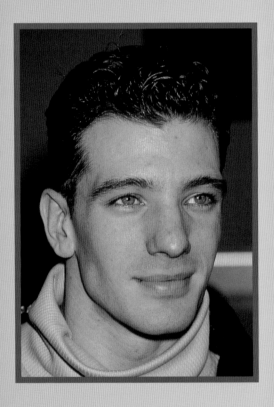

A young JC sports a George Clooney-cropped cut and an adorable smile. While it is true that JC has never had an awkward phase, he has gone through way-cute and cute-but-not-as-cute stages. Early on, it seems like JC wasn't really that concerned with having a style of his own. Here, he might as well be any guy in your history class. And while those big ears are one of JC's sexiest assets, they could benefit from a better haircut.

JC grows his hair out a bit and discovers styling gel. As 'N Sync becomes more and more a part of the popular consciousness, each of the guys has started to explore and develop his own identity within the group. So while Chris is growing his dreads, and Justin is shaving his curly locks, then letting them grow, then cutting them again, and Joey is experimenting with color, JC is just hanging back and keeping it real.

An experiment as rough-edged rocker goes awry. Okay, I am not at all saying that JC isn't totally hot all the time, but there are some looks that suit him better than others. Facial hair and JC are just not a match made in heaven—that goatee hides his gorgeous chiseled cheeks and makes him look much too skinny. Not to mention serious!

and Now

The classic JC. Longish hair, slightly tousled and spiked up with gel. Clean-shaven so he's not hiding those amazing good looks. A black shirt sets off his gorgeous light blue eyes.

Spiked, highlighted, and goateed, JC is almost a mirror image of Sugar Ray frontman Mark McGrath. But what's he praying for?

THEY WRITE THE SONGS—AND PRODUCE THEM TOO!

'N Sync is comprised of five talented guys, all of whom love to write and play their own music. And a few of the guys have started to produce other acts as well.

JC is an all-around music guy. He loves to sing, but he also loves to play and write music! JC has written and co-written countless songs for 'N Sync, even though only some appear on the albums. "We always over-record before we cut an album," he says. "We'll double the amount of songs that go on an album, and then we'll pick what stays and what goes." What did JC write or co-write for No Strings Attached? "Space Cowboy," "No Strings Attached," "Digital Get Down," and "Bringin' Da Noise."

Which of the other guys is starting to try out his producer's wings? How about Lance Bass, the group's resident businessman. Through his management company, Free Lance Entertainment (yes, very cute play on words, Lance!), Lance is managing the careers of at least two clients: Jack Defayo and Meredith Edwards. Lance says, "They're country crossovers, kind of like Shania [Twain]." This is not surprising, considering Lance's love for country music.

Joey has expressed interest in helping other acts, but at the time of this writing, he seems to be figuring out just how. And while Chris has written some songs, he basically has his hands full with FuMan Skeeto, his clothing line.

And speaking of having your hands full, between trying to scrape up a little time for Britney, his family, writing songs for 'N Sync (he helped write "I'll Be Good for You" on No Strings Attached), and all kinds of charity work, Justin hardly has time to breathe—let alone give another act the right kind of attention. But that doesn't mean there isn't a producer in the family. Justin's mom, Lynn Harless, has been trying her hand at managing acts, namely the all-girl group, Innosence.

called the "daddy" of the group, for he's the one who is most likely to look after the other guys (and remind everyone to be on time). But does that mean that he has the tendency to be moody and a sourpuss? Heck no! On the contrary, he very much enjoys going out and having fun with the rest of the gang, and he has a wacky sense of humor too. In fact, the raunchy South Park is his favorite animated show! Having the ability to know when to be serious and when to be fun loving is just one of the many traits that make JC so irresistible!

The guy who has everything must have tripped himself up at times, right? Yes, he admits that he's had more than his share of embarrassing moments. Once, after playing in a charity bowling tournament (yes, that's right—the man plays the old ten-pin) run by Los Angeles Lakers superstar Kobe Bryant, JC went to the parking lot to sign autographs; he was halfway back to his hotel before he realized he was still wearing those geeky bowling shoes.

Is JC still a virgin? To that question, he coyly replies, "I'm a gentleman." And a true gentleman he is, in all his pursuits—romantic, business, and otherwise. He believes in the power of hard work and perseverance, but he doesn't let all his success go to his head. "There's a fine line between conceit and confidence," says JC. He has respect for everyone and is cool to his fans. There is just something about him that is really approachable.

Though not overly romantic in a flowers-and-chocolate kind of way, he does seem like he's somebody who would listen to you and, being as mature and down-to-earth as he is, give you good advice. He comes across as being the kind of guy you'd be thrilled to bring home to meet mom and dad, and it's apparent that he would be that way

even if he wasn't one of the most famous people in the world! But gold-diggers beware. "Spending big bucks is not the way to impress a girl," says JC. Well, I'm sure he knows exactly what does impress a girl. Just look at how many of us are so head-over-heels without ever even having met him—let alone having dated him!

Can you imagine JC as a husband and father? You might not be too far off—though you'll have to wait a while to snag this babe. "I like working and living it as it comes and I don't want to put a schedule on it [marriage], any time frame," he says. "It's just not my style. Hopefully, if I'm inspired to do it at one point, I'll do it."

So yes, we all know that he's super talented and an absolute sweetie, but let's face it: he's also a total hottie! Those sparkling eyes, that stunning smile, and those dazzling cheek-bones. Although he thinks his arms and chest are too skinny, is anybody out there complain-ing? Didn't think so! In fact, when JC was rocking spiky hair, a soul patch, and hip shades at

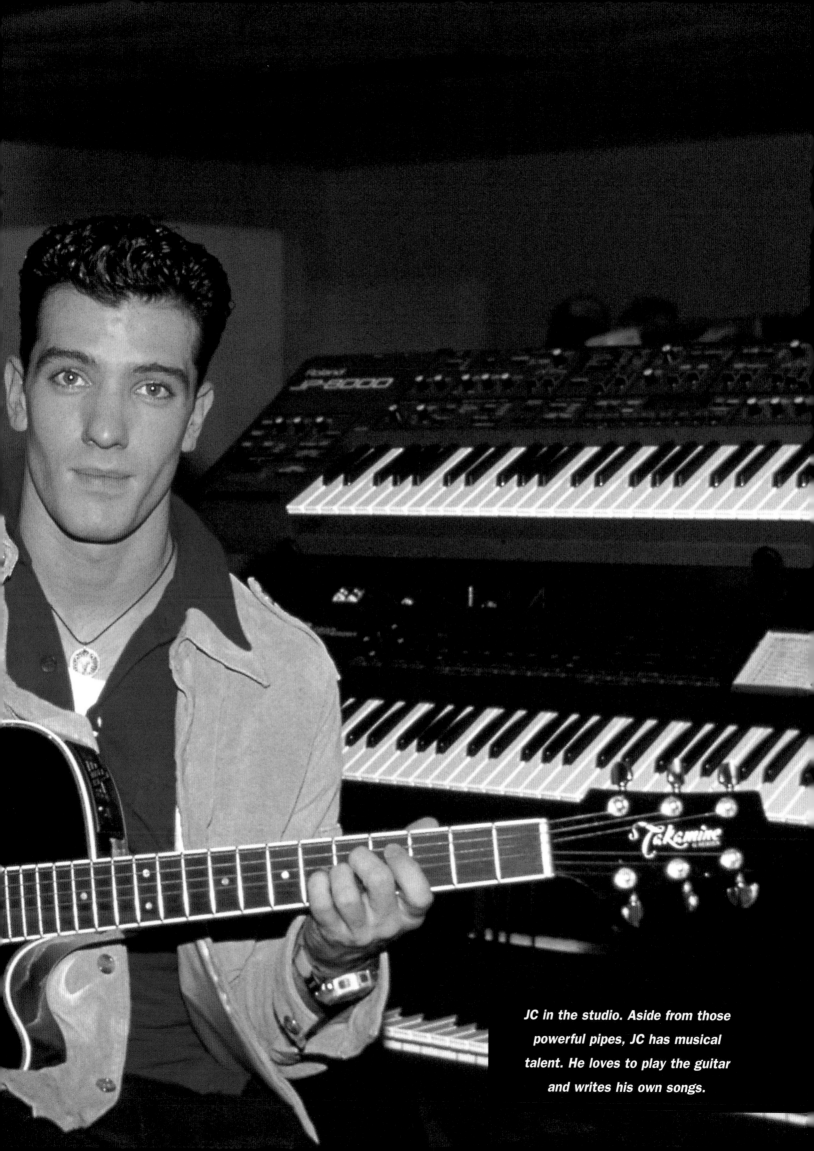

JC in the studio. Aside from those powerful pipes, JC has musical talent. He loves to play the guitar and writes his own songs.

the 2000 Grammys, he looked like he was on his way to a catwalk instead of an awards show! And I'm sure a lot of us remember how adorable he was on the *New Mickey Mouse Club*. This is a man who never went through an awkward phase, that's for sure!

So what does the future hold for Mr. Chaaa-zsayy? You don't need a crystal ball to know that it's going to be brighter than ever—both in front of the spotlight and behind the scenes! Not only is he going to lend an even bigger hand to writing new songs for the much-anticipated follow-up to *No Strings Attached*, but expect to see him collaborate with other artists as well. He has already worked with TLC's Lisa "Left Eye" Lopes on "Space Cowboy" and he co-wrote lots of songs for up-and-coming artists. It wouldn't be a surprise if one day he becomes one of the most sought-after writers and producers in the music industry—from the looks of it, he's already on his way! What words of wisdom can he share with aspiring superstars (and regular folks alike)? "Treat people the way you want to be treated!"

So that's JC Chasez. He has worked his way to the top with the rest of 'N Sync, and with his talent, ambition, and charm, there is no doubt that he will remain there for a long time to come. Stay tuned!

JC strikes a pose during a rehearsal break for the 1999 Golden Globe Awards.

JC Chasez croons during a "Music With a Message: World AIDS Day" performance.

'N Sync gave a killer performance singing the National Anthem at the Jayson Williams Celebrity Softball Challenge in New Jersey, July 2000.

Hey, sexy—if only we all looked so good first thing in the morning!

And with all those special qualities, Justin can sure have his pick of babes. He's never minded casual dating because of his hectic schedule, but what he really loves is to be involved with someone for the long term. L-O-V-E is not taken lightly with the crown prince of pop music, so when he gives himself to a special girl, he gives himself with his whole heart. "When I fall for somebody, I fall hard," says Justin. "It takes a lot for me to fall for someone, but when I do, it's over, that's when I give them everything."

So with all that going for him, who would ever guess that our Justin has ever been in a relationship with a woman who wanted it to *END?* Well, it's true. Justin admits that, "Every relationship I've been in, I've eventually overwhelmed the girl because they just can't handle all the love." What's up with those girls? Couldn't handle the love? Would we ever complain? I think not!

But Cupid has recently struck his arrow through the heart of the right girl. Who has captured the heart of the boy who captured the heart of the entire world? Only a certain young lady named Britney Spears. Who would not be jealous of such a stunning couple? How amazing did those two

Justin: Head to Toe

"I'm charismatic, charming, sincere, and silly." —JUSTIN TIMBERLAKE

Justin has a style all his own, but if there's one word you could use to describe it, it would be CASUAL. Let's break it down:

Justin's trademark is his curly blond hair, though he usually likes to keep it short or tucked away under a hat!

A football jersey is definitely a Justin fashion statement—especially one from one of his fave teams, the San Francisco 49ers.

Justin's bright eyes and full lips have captured the attention of more women than his beloved Britney.

Like we would ever forget their name!

Like most of his 'N Sync buddies, Justin likes to wear his pants loose and comfortable—and why not, with all the dancing he does!

Justin's arms are tight and muscular—no doubt from all the basketball he plays.

Sneakers are a staple of the sporty/casual wardrobe—and Justin wears them as often as he can!

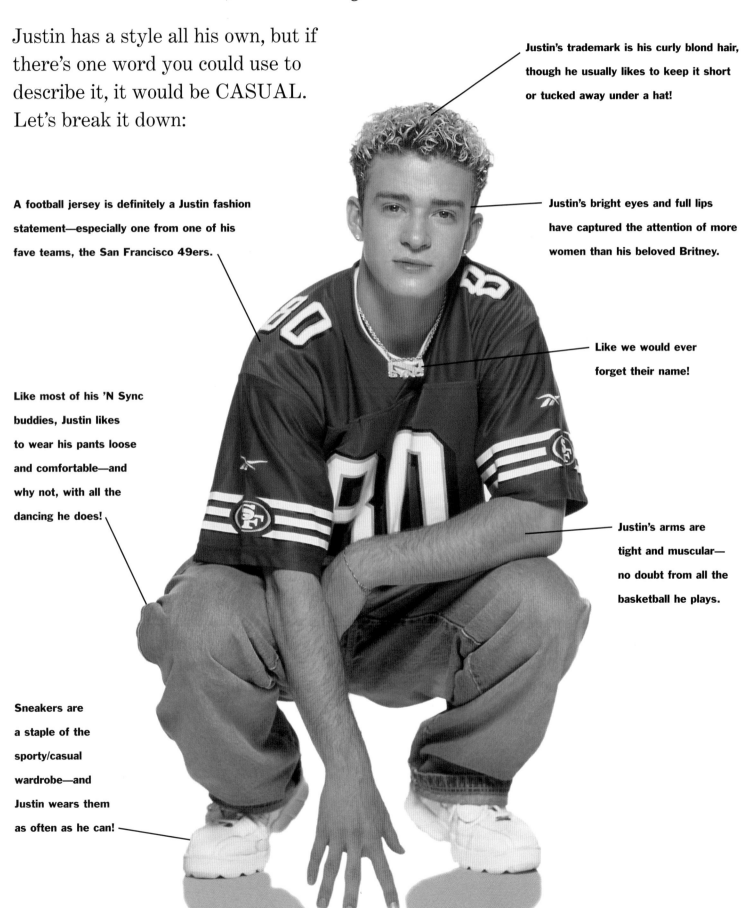

look together at the MTV Music Video Awards and at the VH-1 My Music Awards? They are the prom king and queen of the pop world, that's for sure!

And honestly, with a beau like Justin, Britney's name might as well be "Lucky" after all. For one thing, he's a self-professed total romantic. And it looks like he has met his match in Brit. They both share solid values that keep them grounded and level-headed even while achieving the heights of fame. Justin considers himself to be a very spiritual person, and so does Britney. So as beautiful and glamorous as they are—together and on their own—it's obvious that they really care for each other, and that's what truly counts. Remember how he surprised Britney by bringing her out on stage and serenading her when 'N Sync performed a show that fell on her nineteenth birthday? Insert romantic sigh.

Britney is deliriously happy—and she better not break his heart! Somehow, this seems pretty unlikely. The best thing about their romance is that it's based on a solid friendship—years of working together and knowing each other is what brought them together, not a casual attraction. Britney says about her relationship with Justin, "When you're comfortable with someone you love, the silence is the best. And that's how me and J. are. When we're in a room together, we don't have to say anything. It's for real."

Britney has long professed that she will remain a virgin until her wedding night. You go, girl! And, apparently—guy. Justin and Britney share many of the same values, and Justin is not afraid to admit that the big "S" is not what drives him in a relationship. "I have the opportunity that most guys would kill for", he says of being

Justin gets down performing at the Today show in New York's Rockefeller Center.

10 THINGS YOU MUST KNOW ABOUT JUSTIN

1. He's in love with Britney Spears (so if you're not the jealous type, keep reading!)

2. He's a connoisseur of cereal—Apple Jacks and Cap'n Crunch are his faves.

3. His fave color is baby blue.

4. He collects sneakers.

5. He hates his curly hair.

6. He *loves* chocolate chip ice cream.

7. His favorite ride at Disney World is Space Mountain.

8. His most prized possession is his voice.

9. He shared his first "real" kiss at age thirteen with a girl named Mindy who worked with him at Universal Studios.

10. He's a virgin—and plans to stay a virgin until his wedding night!

Thank goodness it's only a costume! Justin performs during 'N Sync's 2000 world tour.

Evolution of a Style:
Justin, Then

Let's face it—Justin is still a baby compared to the rest of his 'N Sync pals. But he's sure had plenty of different looks in his young life. And I'm just talking hair! He's let it run dirty blond and curly. He's worn a skullcap to hide it. He's even cropped it really short and dyed it bright blond! Watch Justin grow up from a cutie little boy to the sexiest guy under twenty-five in a recent *Teen People* poll.

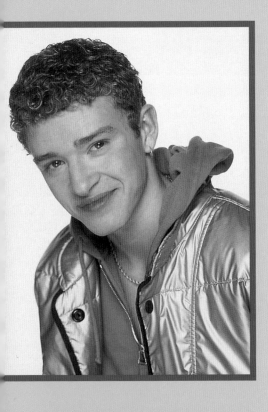

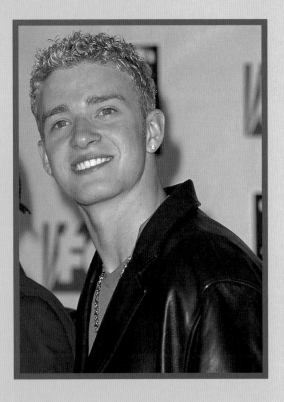

Justin sported a dirty-blond shortish 'do in his early days in the public eye. As his hair is his least-favorite attribute (God only knows why—does he know how much women pay for such sexy curls?!?!?), Justin usually likes to keep it cropped short or tucked under a hat. Looks like he just pulled the hat off for this photo!

Feeling a bit more confident about his curly locks, Justin decided to emphasize his hair by dying it a bright blond. Do blonds have more fun, Justin? More mature, and more comfortable with his looks, Justin exudes a new confidence that makes him even sexier!

Once he colored the hair, and he got more comfortable with it, he must have decided, "Okay. I can do this. The hair is cool. Let's have more!" And so it grew. Add to those long blond curls a sly smile and stylish suit and tie and what do you get? Full-fledged hottie.

and Now

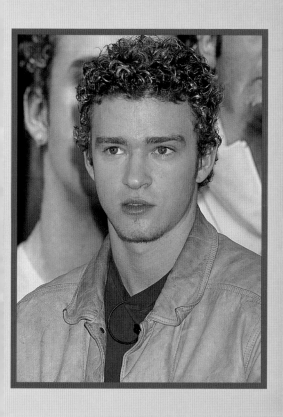

Even when he looks like a doofus, he's irresistible. Eventually, Justin returned to his dark blond roots and opted for a shorter cut, one that let more of his adorable ears peek through and uncovered more of his face. The height of his hair brings more attention to the contours of his face and the fullness of those way-kissable lips!

Okay, so he still has that adorable little-boy face. But what's with this 'do? Through the years, it seems like the wild guys in the band have gotten more conservative, while the conservative guys have gone nuts trying to shake up their clean-cut images. These days, Justin's been known to sport Snoop Dog-style corn rows.

*N SYNC: THE GIFT THAT JUST KEEPS GIVING

How often do you turn on the news and see another story about a celebrity who has so much influence and so much money, yet all he can manage to do is get himself into fix after fix? Well, you'll never hear a report like that about our boys.

All-around good guys—good-looking, good-natured, and good intentioned—'N Sync doesn't waste their surplus cash on partying and getting into trouble. They give of themselves to charity—both money and time—which, if you've ever looked at an 'N Sync tour schedule, you know is more valuable than money!

So far, Chris and Justin have emerged as the group's top philanthropists. Justin has established his own charity, The Justin Timberlake Foundation, to help preserve music education in public schools, while Chris was named national spokesman for Child Watch, an organization devoted to finding missing children. But it doesn't stop there. Here are some more charities and charitable events where Justin and his 'N Sync brothers have stepped in to make a difference:

* *'N Sync's Challenge for the Children, a charity basketball tournament.*

* *Kobe Bowl, basketball star Kobe Bryant's charity bowling tournament (where JC forgot about his shoes!)*

* *Nickelodeon's Annual Big Holiday Help-a-thon, which supports more than twenty charities, including Habitat for Humanity and the March of Dimes*

* *VH-1's Save the Music Campaign*

* *The Teen Harmony Rally in Boston, a protest against discrimination, racism, and hatred*

* *The Stars in the Wild project*

the significant other of Brit-Brit, "but it's all about love for me." Sigh. They just don't make a lot of men like this! It shows how truly special Sir Justin really is. "I want to marry a girl who shares the same values I do," he says. "I have a lot of friends who messed up their lives because they couldn't keep it zipped." Amen. In fact, Justin says, "I'm probably the only guy my age I know who's a virgin, and that's okay by me."

But as serious as they may be about each other, Justin and Britney don't have plans to wed any time soon—so stop believing the rumors. Both are very happy being together now, but almost more importantly, they are devoting as much time as they can to their careers. Justin would like to have kids one day. He believes he had a very good upbringing, one that has really given him the tools he needs to be a good daddy. Oh, but wouldn't Britney and Justin have such beautiful babies together? We'll leave the baby thing up to another 'N Syncer for now...

So what else do we love about Justin? Well, his goofy antics on stage and during interviews are so cute! He's got a great sense of humor, and isn't his "human beatbox" simply da bomb? His joy at being able to entertain is absolutely infectious, and that's one of the best things about Justin. He knows that he was given this great opportunity to share his talent and joy with the world, and is relishing it. You can just tell that he's having the time of his life right now, and that's absolutely endearing.

Even though he has admitted to being a huge procrastinator, Justin is no slacker. He's extremely serious about his craft. After all, he considers his voice to be his most prized possession, so he works hard to keep it in top form. In fact, he considers singing and dancing to be his hobbies, even when he's not performing. What a trooper, huh?

Justin Timberlake and Britney Spears— pop music's cutest couple!

Also, even though Justin has come a long way from performing on *Star Search* in a ten-gallon hat and appearing on the *New Mickey Mouse Club*, you get the sense that he's still the same sweet kid with a huge heart from Memphis, Tennessee. He might be a superstar, but one doubts that he will ever give up his Cap'n Crunch for caviar. And the more famous he becomes, the more generous he gets. Just look at what he's done by establishing the Justin Timberlake Foundation, donating his name and time to a charitable foundation that helps schools create music programs. And even with a whirlwind schedule that consists of traveling around the world performing in front of thousands of adoring fans, he found the time not only to get his high school diploma, but to do so with high grades. Way to go, Justin! Seems like the guy has got brains and looks.

And speaking of his looks—how 'bout that bod? One has to wonder if tank tops weren't created with him in mind. Hey, he's earned it! Despite a professed weakness for chocolate chip ice cream, Mr. Timberlake is Mr. Health Nut. He eats right, never skips breakfast, and hates cigarettes. With habits like these, is it any wonder that he looks so good?

"It's gonna be me!"

But it's not just good food choices that keep this babe lean and svelte. Justin is very active, and spends as much time as he can on the basketball court. He's the best roundball player in the band— even if he isn't the tallest! (Actually, at 5'11", Justin's right smack in the middle of the 'N Sync growth chart—in between Joey and JC, both of whom tower over everyone else at 6'1", and Lance and Chris, 5'10" and 5'8" respectively.) I wonder how he'd fare in a one-on-one match with Brian Littrell of the Backstreet Boys, who's that band's resident basketball nut—and lead singer. Hmmm. A new twist in the battle of the boy bands.

Battle of the bands or not, where does Justin want to see the group in the coming years? He wants the guys and their music to grow up and evolve with the fan group they have right now, in the same way that Madonna's fans grew up with her. "We want to evolve with the crowd that's with us right now," he says, "and hopefully they'll stay with us."

Ultimately, for Justin, it all comes back to the fact that underneath that gorgeous exterior there is this guy with a big heart and a beautiful voice. Is it any wonder that we love Justin so?

Justin smiles during a 1999 performance at New York's Nassau Coliseum.

Piano man Justin Timberlake tickles the ivories in the studio.

Ladies and gentlemen!
'N Troducing the Jackson 5!

CHAPTER THREE

Whole Lotta Lance

> SWM, early 20s. Taurus. Seeks eventual long-term relationship/marriage with a special someone who is straightforward, sweet, and not outspoken. She can be a fan—but she has to be down to earth. Also, she should be open to having children—and to unusual names for said children, like Xander. Enjoys the beach, horseback riding, and quiet time. Loudmouths need not apply.

Can cutie Lance Bass be summed up in one word? Maybe not one, but perhaps four: practical, businesslike, down-to-earth (okay, so that's three words in itself!), and adorable, natch!

Lance is practical because he likes to think before he acts, whether he's writing a song or approaching a girl for a date. In fact, his 'N Sync pals have lovingly bestowed upon him the nickname "Stealth" because of this. The guys really love to tease him about this. Joey says "Lance uses us like wild dogs…he holds us by the leash and waits for us to sniff people out and then he goes and meets them himself."

Lance Bass looking hot at the 2001 Sundance Film Festival.

Not to say that he's shy, though. Lance is one of the chattiest members of the fivesome, but he likes to take his time, go over what he's going to say, and then speak his mind, politely and tactfully. To know Lance, there's no doubt why he earned the "If you're looking for a guy to have sparring matches with, you're going to have to look elsewhere, ladies!" endorsement.

If, of course, you're looking for a man who's going to take good care of you and make sure you're treated right, then Lance Bass may very well be your man. And good news: he has no objection to dating fans—you just have to be the right kind of fan. His criteria are simple: he's looking for a girl who knows what she wants but isn't bossy about it. In fact, he really doesn't want to marry anyone "in the business." So that means more chances for us, right? Really all he needs is

Lance: Head to Toe

"When we first met him, that boy had those little preppy button shirts… Have you ever seen those haircuts where they put bowls over your head and cut around it? That's what Lance's hair looked like." —JOEY ON LANCE

Lance has a classic style. There's not much improving you can do with blue eyes, blond hair, and flawless skin—right? Clothing-wise, Lance likes the basics: a comfy pair of jeans—or overalls— a T-shirt or sweatshirt, weather permitting.

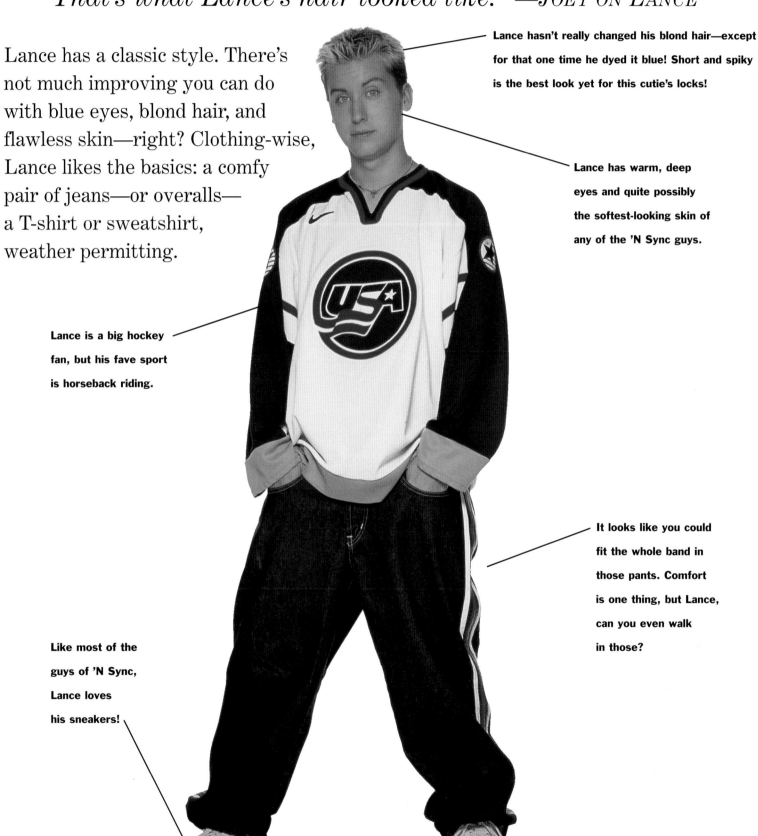

Lance hasn't really changed his blond hair—except for that one time he dyed it blue! Short and spiky is the best look yet for this cutie's locks!

Lance has warm, deep eyes and quite possibly the softest-looking skin of any of the 'N Sync guys.

Lance is a big hockey fan, but his fave sport is horseback riding.

It looks like you could fit the whole band in those pants. Comfort is one thing, but Lance, can you even walk in those?

Like most of the guys of 'N Sync, Lance loves his sneakers!

"...someone I can have fun with, someone I can laugh with and I see myself having two kids [with]—a boy and a girl," he says.

So it looks like marriage is in the cards for this cutie... Now if only he can hold down a long-term relationship, he'll be set. Not being able to be seriously involved with someone rates right up there with not being able to see his family as much as he'd like. "I see it [marriage] for myself when I'm older, maybe late twenties," says Lance. "I probably would marry in my early twenties if I wasn't in 'N Sync." Hold on, Lance! You'll find the right girl, one who won't mind sharing you with the rest of the world!

And when Lance does finally settle down, will it be in the house he recently purchased in Mississippi? Could be. The house was only a year old when he bought it, but perfectionist that he is, Lance had it re-modeled to suit his tastes. He even built a lake in the back so he can jet ski! What's in his house? One of his favorite rooms is his Dr. Seuss room, which features three original works by the children's book master. But ask him what his favorite thing about his house is, and he'll tell you it's the *Star Wars* virtual reality pinball machine he likes to play whenever he has the time. "You'd have to see it," he gushes. "It's amazing." Yes, Lance, we're sure it is!

Lance the businessman started his own entertainment management company called, fittingly, Free Lance Entertainment. On top of his business pursuits, Lance is really psyched about writing his own songs. He wrote

Although he's performing at the Today *show in this shot, Lance really looks like he's dreaming about what to have for lunch.*

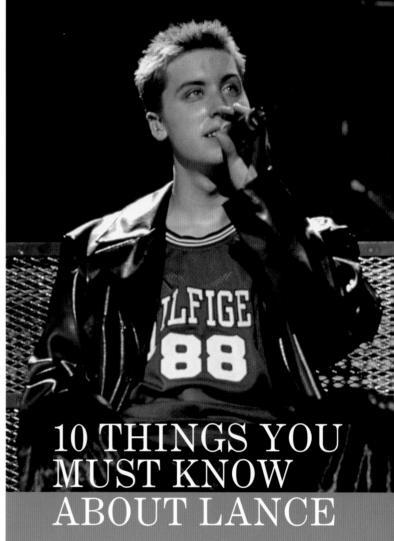

10 THINGS YOU MUST KNOW ABOUT LANCE

1. His real name is James.

2. He was the last guy to join 'N Sync.

3. He considers himself a proper southern gentleman.

4. He is the most business-minded guy in the group.

5. He wants the group to still be together in twenty years—making music, making movies, making money, and just having a GREAT time!

6. Some day he wants to design a roller coaster.

7. He loves *I Love Lucy* reruns!

8. His fave place to get away from it all is the beach.

9. He appeared on *7th Heaven*, playing Lucy's love interest—and will be returning to that role soon!

10. He's the WORST basketball player in the group—and quite possibly, the world. This doesn't bother him, though. He knows he's great at lotsa other things!

Evolution of a Style:
Lance, Then

Proper southern gentleman, indeed—Lance has never been one to reach for the hair dye or get a tattoo, although he did once dye the tips of his hair blue for a concert. Needless to say, this was not popular with fans, so he won't be going back to that look anytime soon. Here's a rundown:

No one in the band has changed as much as Lance—without changing his style at all. When Lance first joined the band, he looked about ten years old—well, maybe eleven! But oh, how he's grown!

Someone must have told Lance somewhere down the line that bangs make you look younger than you are, so eventually, he decided to grow them out and spike them up with the rest of his hair—a great style choice that has become Lance's trademark look.

Is Lance a natural blond? The roots tell a different story—unless he decided to touch them up to create a 'do with more dimension. Whatever the case, the dark roots gave Lance's image more grit and character, making this baby-faced popster look a bit more mature.

and Now

Lance has admitted that he likes his conservative look best, but sometimes he experiments in Chris-and-Joey-land. A cutoff jean jacket and shades is a great look for some, but somehow, it just doesn't seem like Lance.

Lance Bass today, totally into his style and totally loving life. The blond spikes over dark roots has proven to be the best look for him and he wears it well—whether long or short. And how he's grown into those good looks!

ALL THAT AND A SIDE OF LANCE

They say the way to a man's heart is through his stomach—but who are they kidding with that, girlfriends? We all know that one of the best ways a man can prove himself worthy of our love is to show us that he knows his way around the kitchen—or at least try to find his way!

Did you know that Lance actually prides himself on whipping up original culinary treats when he has the time? Just one of the many reasons that this 'N Sync hottie is definitely one to snare!

Some of Lance's favorite concoctions center around the most important course—dessert! In fact, you can even find one of his recipes on Teenmag.com. The tasty treat they write about is a yummy, chocolately, cheese-cakey thing called "Lance's Chocolate Dream." Who would have guessed that our boy Lance would know how to put a bit of cream cheese, chocolate pudding, whipped topping, almonds, and pecans (southern pecans, of course) into such a tasty treat? Even if you happen to be dieting right now, you've got to try it out. It's the only way to find out if Lance will know just the right way to top off the romantic dinner he prepares for you in one of your Valentine's Day reveries. It's at least one way to have a piece of Lance right in your own home!

Truly a kid at heart, Lance clowns around in a hotel room on tour.

three songs for *No Strings Attached*, but it was too late
for them to be included. He's not worried and is sure
that at least one will appear on the new album. Hope so!

Lance is really inspired by other musicians, and one of
the best things about being with 'N Sync is that he gets to work with so many talented
people, like Phil Collins, with whom 'N Sync recorded a song for the *Tarzan* soundtrack. "Phil
was very great, very down to earth," Lance remembers. "It was really cool, cause nothing
was set in the song, it was all scatting. So the six of us went in and just scatted and whatever
was recorded was left in."

Lance chills out at home—a place he wishes he could see more.

Another perk of stardom: the fans' antics. One time, a fan threw a bra on stage and Joey put it on the drummer's head. Lance loved this, and he admits that among his fave things that fans throw onstage are bras and panties. Don't get any crazy ideas, ladies. Wait a minute! I thought that Lance was Mr. Gentleman! Well, I guess we all have our weaknesses!

Lance sees a lot more acting in his future. He had a great response from his performance playing opposite Beverly Mitchell on 7*th* *Heaven*— and will be reprising that role soon for at least two shows. It was the first kiss for Beverly's character Lucy. So were there any sparks? Maybe under different circumstances, but Lance says of Beverly, "She's a great kisser, but it was an acting kiss. It's weird when there's fifty people watching you." Lance is no stranger to romance with TV stars. He did date *Boy Meets World*'s Danielle Fischel, after all!

The last member to join 'N Sync, Lance's vocal stylings and business sense have been a huge asset to the band's success, in the past, present, and definitely in the future! And speaking of the future, what does Lance see for the guys? Staying together, that's what! "I mean if the Rolling Stones can do it, we can do it." Hear, hear!

Lance Bass shows off some of his group's accomplishments.

"Hey! Am I the coolest 'N Syncer or what?!?"

The guys of 'N Sync prove that each band member has a style of his own at the MTV Movie Awards.

CHAPTER FOUR

Crushin' on Chris

SWM, Libra, pushing 30. Seeks a woman who doesn't obsess over marriage, who is free-spirited and knows how to have fun without money. Enjoys chocolate milk, collecting records, and writing songs. Most important aspect in a potential mate: compatibility.

Chris Kirkpatrick marches to the beat of his own drum, and we all adore him for that. Okay, so the braids weren't exactly the best of looks, but we all forgive him. Once he chopped those snakes off his scalp, he began to rival Justin and even JC for the romantic attention of the fans—at least for this fan! But did he do it because he didn't like the way they looked? Not really. They just got in the way. Says Chris, "…when I took a shower I had to wash each one. It took like eight hours to get them re-braided." Hassle or not, good riddance to the mop!

An even sexier self-improvement came when Chris decided to get braces. It happened just a short time

Chris Kirkpatrick performs in Houston, Texas, in the summer of 1999.

after starting with the band. At first he thought they were really going to get in the way. I guess most people were so fixated on that hair, they never even noticed the tin grin! But they notice that sweet, straight smile now—well worth the time behind bars, and an inspiration to those of us still wearing them ourselves!

What can we say? Chris is his own guy. He knows what he wants and he goes after it. After all, wasn't it Chris who started 'N Sync when he was getting tired of waiting for his big break?

He's the resident comedian. He's the one who screams about trees during an AOL chat session, when everyone else is answering questions from fans. He's the one who makes wise cracks and blames it on his fellow 'N Syncers. The oldest of all the guys, he sometimes acts like their ten-year-old kid brother—but they wouldn't have it any other way. "I'm pretty much the

Chris: Head to Toe

"A bag of fleas is easier to control than our dear Chris Kirkpatrick" —JC ON CHRIS

Chris defines 'N Sync style, looking sizzlin' all dressed up or in his wackiest getup. It's no wonder he's the 'N Syncer with his own fashion line!

At last, Chris has shorn his dreads, allowing us to focus on his cutie-pie face and not what he's doing with his hair!

Born in 1971, Chris is the oldest member of 'N Sync—and by more than a couple of years. You could never tell by looking at him, though, with that adorable baby face!

As creator of his own clothing line, FuMan Skeeto, Chris is always looking to shake things up with his outfits. While most of the guys are comfortable slumming around in sports jerseys, sweatshirts, and tank tops, Chris is only happy when he wears something that stands out.

The perfect complement to a silver vest? Why, black baggy pants—natch!

Clunky black shoes are Chris's footwear of choice—except, of course, for the hi-tops he wears on the basketball court or perhaps a pair of rollerblades!

most immature," Chris explains, "...so I usually go to them for advice and they tell me to settle down."

Chris also has a huge sense of adventure. One time he surfed in a hurricane. (It won't be anytime soon before he tries that again.) As a daring and creative spirit, Chris is someone who loves to try new things and isn't afraid to take risks. In fact, he just started his own clothing line! Now, while we all know that Chris is a great performer, how many of us know what a smart businessman he is as well. Chris? Yes. Chris Kirkpatrick of 'N Sync? Yes. A businessman?? Y-E-S—and a successful one to boot. His clothing line, FuMan Skeeto, specializes in funky streetwear, mostly geared toward women at the time of this writing—but he's looking forward to getting into men's clothes soon. He's even started designing for the other guys in the band. As reported to Teenmag.com, "...we've created a Superman-symbol-looking thing for Joey [Fatone]. We're creating some bandanas for Justin [Timberlake], a bunch of different stuff for each of the guys."

So who would Chris most like to dress? Without hesitation, Chris says Gwen Stefani. Why? Cuz, as he says, "She's got the style." And, of course, he's got a huge crush on her, which doesn't hurt!

So what does Chris look for in a girl—other than perhaps that she be Gwen Stefani? Lots of things. He likes free spirits, like himself. He likes women who don't expect to be lavished with expensive gifts—girls who know how to enjoy themselves, and him, without

Chris sings at New York's Jingle Ball 1998.

10 THINGS YOU MUST KNOW ABOUT CHRIS

1. He's the founder of 'N Sync.

2. He thinks his feet are too BIG!

3. His fave food is Mexican.

4. He studied psychology in school.

5. He's terrified of getting married—even though at the time of this writing, he's been involved with his "secret sweetheart" for over a year.

6. He says he has a very short attention span.

7. His prized possession is an autographed photo of Bruce Lee.

8. He's the oldest member of the band (Chris turned 30 on October 17, 2001).

9. He's a video-game junkie.

10. He wore braces—and only got them when he was in his late twenties. You think you have it bad!!

Evolution of a Style:
Chris, Then

For a long time, Chris was the most recognizable member of 'N Sync. What with those streaming dreadlocks—who could miss him? But he's moved on to more updated 'dos, and he's all the sexier for it. Here's a survey of Chris as he makes his way from moptop to full-fledged hottie:

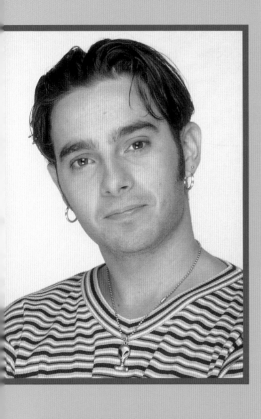  

Pre-dreadlock Chris looking sweet and innocent. Maybe this is why he grew those darn things—he needed an edge. Completely devoid of facial hair and wearing only three earrings, to look at this photo you would never suspect the Chris that was to come.

Holy transformation, Batman! Amazing how a mop of dreads can transform a guy from clean-cut preppie to radical bad-boy! Of course, a long leather jacket never hurt either!

Chris pulls the mop into a high ponytail and adds more beads. Notice how in just about every early pic you see of Chris, he's smiling with his mouth closed? That's cuz if he opened that mouth, he'd be showing off that old tin grin!

and Now

The braces come off and, oh, what a difference they made! There are few things in life sexier than a smiling Chris Kirkpatrick—and when that smile is full of perfectly straight pearly whites... it makes a girl swoon. Glasses, facial hair, jewelry, and those dreads—now minus the beads—compete his pop-star look.

Bye bye bye dreads and hello babe! Even though Chris says he cut his hair because it was a hassle to take care of, he must know how much sexier he looks with short, spiky hair. He looks just like the little cutie-pie he started out as, only now he's more rugged and manly. Ooo la la!

THE PRICE OF FAME

'N Sync broke the Backstreet Boys' record sales for Millennium—and in one day! While all the guys love their fame, it comes with its drawbacks. What about the lawsuit a fan took up against Justin and the rest of the guys because he didn't pay her enough attention—and then she alleged that he verbally abused her? And believe it or not, all of the guys have been suffering some hearing loss, and it's not from all the loud music. "We had a doctor a couple of years ago say that our ears are going bad because there's a certain pitch that those girls send out that will deafen you," admits Lance. But don't worry—scream loud and proud when you see these babes because they've found a way to deal with the sitch. "...we have these in-ear monitors now that block out most of the screaming." So if they don't respond, don't go off and sue them. They love you—they're just trying to save themselves from hearing aids!

What are some of the other casualties of fame? Chris says he never has any privacy, so this hyperactive wild child is forced to stay in a lot because it's too crazy to go out. "A lot of people come up to you and want to be your friend just because you have a name," he says. "You feel like saying 'If I weren't in a group, you wouldn't even be talking to me.' It makes you really weary." Chris has been able to cope somewhat with a disguise: a baseball cap and sunglasses.

Aside from constant recognition, the schedule the N' Syncers have to maintain really takes a toll. Joey hates "Not having any sleep," while JC, who relishes hard work, says the worst part is the grueling travel schedule. Justin hates the lack of privacy and Lance doesn't like that they "...can't go places and just be normal." And all the guys strongly agree on one of the toughest pitfalls of fame: not seeing their family and friends as much as they'd like.

But they wouldn't trade it for anything in the world. Says JC, "We know there's a million other groups out there doing this—we want to be one of the few that are around for a long time."

"I believe I can fly."
Chris Kirkpatrick
shows off one
of his many talents.

a price tag. "I don't like it when they expect stuff and come with demands, that's baloney!" Such strong language, Chris!!!

Chris is a romantic guy, but he's also a serious commitment-phobe, so look out, girls, if you want to grow old with Chris Kirkpatrick! In fact, when asked during an AOL chat about the first thing he looks for in a girl, Chris immediately said, "A way out." How does Chris fall in love? "I look at her eyes, I find a gaze irresistible," he says, and adds that "...the most important thing is her personality and she must be compatible with you. I love it when she can be my best friend."

Chris has been seeing a woman for more than a year, but at this point, the idea of marriage is completely foreign to him. "I can be a one woman guy, but marriage scares me too much. It freaks me out. It's permanent."

No, Chris. It's normal to sleep in your sneakers. Really it is!

Braided on top, and beaded around the neck, Chris knows how to accessorize.

Did you know that this 'N Sync wild child is also a college graduate? It's true. Chris holds a psychology degree from Florida's Rollins University, so despite the zany antics, Chris has proven to be very grounded in his ambitions, and accomplished in all his endeavors. And luckily, his commitment issues don't spill over to his commitment to the group. "I hope we're still being successful [in the coming years]. It'll be on a different level, of course, because every group has to change with the times," he says. "Honestly, I know of groups that are very well looked at in the industry and they started out like us, but over time, they've proven their longevity and hopefully that's what we can accomplish." Will that energy translate into his love life? Only time will tell!

Chris believes in karma. He says that he tries to be nice to everyone he meets and goes out of his way to help people. In March 2000, he was named national spokesperson for Child Watch, an organization devoted to finding missing children. What comes around goes around, and while this isn't why he does all the nice things he does, he admits that "the karmic value, it just comes back to you, it can come back and kick you in the ass."

The guys at the 28th Annual American Music Awards in January 2001.

CHAPTER FIVE

Hot Cuppa Joey

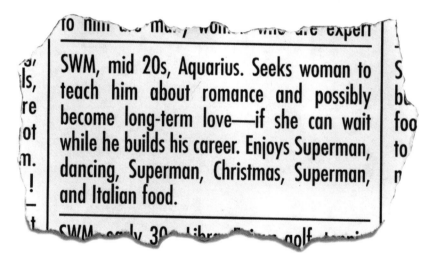

SWM, mid 20s, Aquarius. Seeks woman to teach him about romance and possibly become long-term love—if she can wait while he builds his career. Enjoys Superman, dancing, Superman, Christmas, Superman, and Italian food.

Like his idol, Superman, Joey has soared to great heights in an illustrious career that began innocently enough when he stepped onstage at age seven in a kindergarten production of *Pinocchio*. From that moment, Joey knew that he wanted to perform, and it has been uphill ever since for this Brooklyn-born sweetheart.

And what a performer he is! We all know that he's got pipes that melt hearts, but did you know that Joey is an accomplished tap dancer, and that he had a small role in a film with Robert De Niro when he was a kid? Is this guy a triple-threat or what?

But we all love Joey for more than just his talents. Let's face it, the guy is completely irresistible! He has a warm, friendly smile, fabulously framed by that

**Joey Fatone, Jr,
junk food connoisseur.**

Joey takes a giggle
break during a
rehearsal for a
video shoot.

trademark goatee, and a funky, edgy style all his own. Why, it
seems like he is changing hair color every other week! Let's see,
there were the clean-shaven early days, the naturally brunette
locks over the forehead with the pierced eyebrow, the recent
choppy bleach-blond 'do (complete with roots), and let's not forget that interesting shade
officially known as "Red Corvette"! This is a guy who is not afraid to express himself, that's
for sure!

   One of the coolest things about Joey is that he happens to be a regular nice guy who
loves to go out and have a good time. He's the biggest flirt of the group, and he's the
member of the gang who would most likely be found shakin' his booty 'til the wee hours at
some hot-ticket nightclub. But Joey is no play-uh. He despises phoniness and isn't afraid to

Joey: Head to Toe

"...Joey's very tacky." —Chris on Joey

At one time, he was casual-boy, but that's all changed. He dyed his hair pink and his style followed suit. Now, says Joey, "I sometimes wear weird clothes. Like, I have this pirate's jacket with big fuzzy cuffs." Let's define Joey-style:

These days it seems like Joey changes his hairstyle like he changes his underwear! Despite this, his locks still seem to have a healthy sheen and manageability. I wonder what his secret is?

Joey's face has more character than any other band member's. His looks are rough and manly, but soft underneath. One look into those eyes and you know a sensitive soul lurks within.

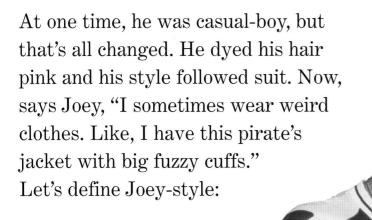

Who would Joey be without his Superman necklace? Since the day he got it, he's never taken it off.

Joey can—and will—wear just about anything he wants. Who else could pull off this wacky shirt decorated with... are those orange lightning bolts?

And those jeans... Joey can, and does, go either way with the pants he wears—baggy or snug, jeans or sweats, long pants or short. Those sexy legs lay the framework and Joey's fashion sense does the rest.

Joey's most comfortable in a pair of sneakers—not surprising for a Brooklyn boy who spends a lot of time shooting hoops on the basketball court.

poke fun at himself. After all, how many heart-throbs do you know of out there who admit to snoring?

In fact, Joey's very down-to-earth about who he is—good points and bad—and who he isn't. He genuinely takes things in his stride. Remember when his pants ripped on *The Rosie O'Donnell Show*? A lesser man may have blushed and tried to pretend it didn't happen. Joey—in typical Joey fashion—confronted the event and laughed about it. "My butt is getting too big," he claimed. "Been eating too many snacky cakes!" And what about all the fun he pokes at himself? "I picked my nose when I was younger, therefore I have big nostrils." Silly boy!

As the group's resident flirt, Joey has surely been attracted to his share of women. So what does he look for? Leggy, busty blonds? Try again. Our man Joey is a man of substance, and for him, "There's nothing more attractive than a girl with a sincere smile." He readily admits: "I'm really attracted to big smiles and confident attitudes."

What kind of boyfriend is Joey? Respectful, honest, and very open. He says that he's not very much of a romantic so he needs a woman who can teach him a thing or two in that department. Joey looks for a girl with beautiful eyes, one who can hang out in sweats and sneakers and still look good. "And when I'm married," says Joey, "I want to be able to wake up next to her and she'll look as beautiful when she wakes up as she did when we went out the night before." Well, we all know about bed head and the havoc that makeup can wreak when it's not properly removed the night before—

Look deeply into my eyes, darling!

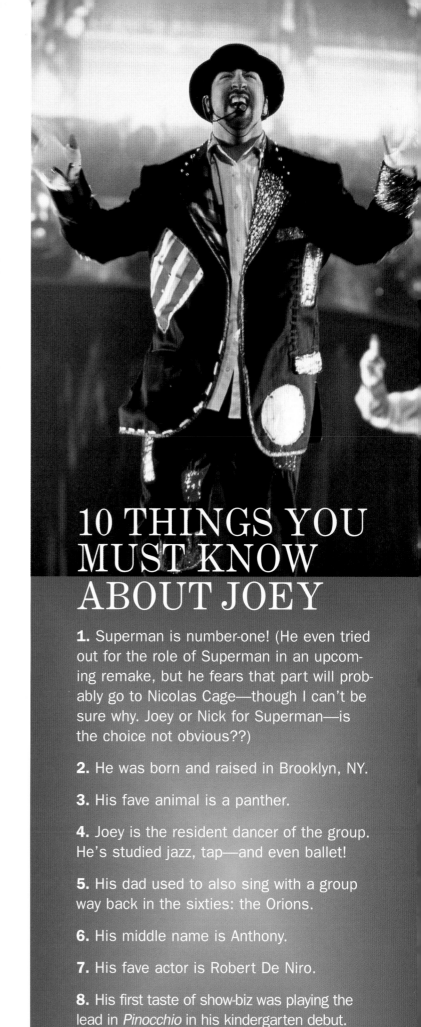

10 THINGS YOU MUST KNOW ABOUT JOEY

1. Superman is number-one! (He even tried out for the role of Superman in an upcoming remake, but he fears that part will probably go to Nicolas Cage—though I can't be sure why. Joey or Nick for Superman—is the choice not obvious??)

2. He was born and raised in Brooklyn, NY.

3. His fave animal is a panther.

4. Joey is the resident dancer of the group. He's studied jazz, tap—and even ballet!

5. His dad used to also sing with a group way back in the sixties: the Orions.

6. His middle name is Anthony.

7. His fave actor is Robert De Niro.

8. His first taste of show-biz was playing the lead in *Pinocchio* in his kindergarten debut.

9. He HATES phonies!

10. Joey wears boxer-briefs from Fruit of the Loom!

Evolution of a Style:
Joey, Then

Next to Chris, Joey is the most standout member of the group for his daring looks—but this wasn't always the case. How has he changed? Let's see:

Straight from his Brooklyn neighborhood and into the role of boy-band heartthrob—Joey made the transition well. With his slicked-back hair and a clean-shaven face, Joey almost looks like a little brother of the Joey we know today.

Joey soon cut his hair and opted for an edgier, spiky look. He replaced his Gap-style wardrobe with lots of black and leather, started to grow his trademark goatee, and look out—the Joey Fatone, Jr, we all know and love today began to emerge.

The goatee begins to take shape— but those shades have got to go! Joey did a lot of experimenting while fine-tuning his recent look, and sometimes he's made better decisions than others!

and Now

Actually, Joey is more of a work in progress than a finished piece. As soon as he realized he could branch out and change his look by changing the color of his hair, all bets were off. Blond hair one day, bright pink the next—for a while it seemed like he was trying to go shade for shade with Gwen Stefani!

The essence of Joey: wacky—not to mention brightly hued—hairdo, lots of leather and jewelry, and lots of facial hair. Joey definitely walks on the wild side!

*N THE MOVIES

You will soon be able to catch the guys on the big screen—and eventually on video and DVD. They recently hooked up with Tom Hanks's production company, and are slated to write, direct, and produce their combined big-screen debut sometime in 2001. (Remember, it's their combined debut, because Joey's already been in movies.)

They will not be playing themselves, but they say they will be starring in the film. "What's really great is, it's an 'N Sync project. It's something that the group is gonna be doing, and it's fun for us," says Lance. "We've got a tremendous budget. We're gonna have some amazing actors. We're hoping that it might be a musical."

If the guys weren't going to act in the film—and if it was, in fact, going to be about them—"casting director" Joey has his ideas on who would play whom:

Justin: *Ryan Phillippe*

Joey: *David Schwimmer*

Chris: *Adam Sandler*

JC: *Luke Perry*

He got stumped on **Lance**... perhaps there's a rising star out there waiting to fill that role?

Sexy, self-assured, and sensitive, Joey will make for a great husband and dad!

so I'm pretty sure this doesn't mean the made-up version of a girl, but the natural one!

The funny thing is, Joey is a romantic, but because it's not in the traditional way, he doesn't really see it. Why do I say this? Joey remembers "falling in love" when he was really young. "I went to my grandmother's over the summer and I kissed a girl," he recalls. "I don't remember her name, but I do remember crying in the shower because I would never see her again." If that's not melt-your-heart romantic, I just don't know what is!!

But alas! Before any of you plan your Joey-snaring strategy and attempt to sign him up for romance lessons, it looks like Joey has apparently found that woman. According to widely circulating rumors, he and his girlfriend are expecting their first baby in the summer of 2001! Of course, this may just be hopeful speculation on the part of a few Joey-obsessed reporters. If it's true, we're very happy for him. After all, he has always said that his plans for the future

BENDABLE FIGURES
WITH ACCESSORIES

BEND & POSE 'EM ANY WAY YOU LIKE

FATONE

FAMILY

Joey's musical pursuits take a backseat to his
fondness for toys and collectibles—
and, of course, to Superman!

include marriage and a family, so it seems that he is well on his way to achieving this goal. But honestly, what goal has he set out to accomplish that he hasn't achieved?

Professionally, he's very pleased with the progress he and the guys have made in the years they've been singing and performing together. And he lets all criticism roll right off his back. "Boy bands? We're not a boy band, he laughs to the harshest critics. "We're more like a dude band."

There's a reason he's earned the rep of being "the friendly one." He loves touring the world and meeting new people and learning all about them. He always goes out of his way to talk to people. "The best part about being on tour is meeting our fans and performing in front of thousands of people," he says. "It's a great feeling to touch so many lives."

And despite all the fame and glory of recent years, Joey swears, "We're still normal guys. It's always fun being recognized and everything, but our feet are always on the ground. What you see is what you get."

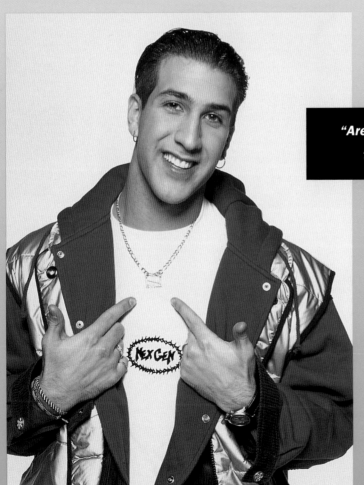

"Are you talkin' ta me?"

Joey works up a sweat at a recent performance.

Who would have figured Lance to be the resident troublemaker of 'N Sync?

'N Sync Resources

'N SYNC FAN CLUB

The 'N Sync Official International Fan Club
P.O.Box 5248
Bellingham, Washington 98227
USA
Contact: Gerri Karr, Fan Club Manager

WEBSITES

Official:
www.nsync.com

Also worth a visit:
www.nsyncheaven.com
www.angelfire.com/music/nsyncplaza/
http://www.angelfire.com/il/
laurennlance/index.html
www.travel.to/n_sync/
www.wallofsound.go.com
www.rollingstone.com
www.billboard.com
There's lots more where that came from. Your best bet is go to one of your favorite search engines, like Yahoo or Lycos, type in "n sync," and a whole world of 'N Sync information will be open to you. Here's a tip: log on with your 'rents when you want to search this stuff out. There's a lot of phony baloney on the Web and your folks can help you get past all that and into the good stuff!

MAGAZINES

Check out these magazines monthly for stories and interviews featuring your favorite boy band!
All-Stars
B.B.
Blast
Cosmo Girl!
Cute
Entertainment Teen

J – 14
Jane
Kickin'
Seventeen
Sixteen
Super Teen
Teen Beat
Teen Celebrity
Teen People

BIBLIOGRAPHY

PERIODICALS

"Last Week's Answer: The U.S. Virgin Islands." *Time for Kids*. (December 18, 1998): 8.

Arnold, Chuck. "Chatter: The screaming of female fans is adversely affecting the hearing of the 'N Sync music group." *People Weekly*. (July 24, 2000): 148.

Christman, Ed and Anna Berent. "Jive's 'N Sync Breaks Records." *Billboard*. (April 1, 2000): 1.

Gadzik, Tanya. "Oxy Balance Gets 'N Sync With Teens." *Brandweek*. (February 15, 1999): 12.

Helligar, Jeremy. "Boy Power: Watch Your Backs, Backstreet Boys! 'N Sync conquers charts—and teenage hearts—with sweet harmonies." *People Weekly*. (February 8, 1999): 93.

Jewel, Dan. "Pop's Puppy Lovers: Ex Mousketeers Britney Spears and 'N Sync's Justin Timberlake get in tune." *People Weekly*. (November 27, 2000): 85.

Johnson, Tricia. "Gimme Shelter: Singer JC Chasez's Hollywood Hills Home." *Entertainment Weekly*. (February 16, 2001): 18.

Laudadio, Marisa. "Catching Up With Justin Timberlake of 'N Sync." *Teen* Magazine. (January 2000): 46.

Laudadio, Marisa. "The Making of 'N Sync's newest video." *Teen* Magazine. (April 2000): 72.

Marron, Maggie. "N Sync." *Kickin'*. (vol 2 no 3).

Paoletta, Michael. "Jive's Plan: 'N Sync Everywhere." *Billboard*. (February 19, 2000): 1.

Pesselnick, Jill. "April Certs Mark Feats By 'N Sync, Dion, Chicks." *Billboard*. (May 13, 2000): 137.

Taylor, Chuck. "N Sync Spends Its 'Time' Evolving Into More Than Just a Teen Pop Sensation." *Billboard*. (November 7, 1998): 104.

Waddell, Ray. "'N Sync In Rhythm: $30 Mil Year Possible For Youth Band." *Amusement Business*. (February 1, 1999): 3.

WORLD WIDE WEB

"'N Sync Expands Horizons With Alabama, Gloria Estefan." Mtv.com
"'N Sync." launch.com
"Which Star Signs Are Compatible?" www.stargazers.com
abstracts.net
agirlsworld.com
fatonezone.com
Gelman, Jason. "Estefan on 'Music' and 'N Sync." Launch.com
mtv.com
nsync.com
nwnsync.com
people.com
rollingstone.com
teenmag.com
yahoo.com (chat)
ymshomepage.com

BOOKS

Marron, Maggie. *The Ultimate 'N Sync Quiz Book*. Metrobooks: New York. 2000.

Martin, Lexi and Jessica Davis. *'N Sync*. Metrobooks: New York. 2000.

'N Sync Backstreet Pass: Your Kickin' Keepsake Scrapbook. Scholastic: New York. 1999.

Nichols, Angie. *'N Sync: Get 'N Sync With the Guys*. Billboard: New York. 1998.

Index

Photo Credits: